A Somber Grimoire – What I'd Tell My Kin I'll Never Have

by: T. F. Lanning

A Somber Grimoire – What I'd Tell My Kin I'll Never Have
Copyright © 2023 by: T. F. Lanning
ISBN: 9798375338026
Printed in the U.S.A.

Rhyme that searches to find its way, telling the kin I'll never have how to help them to better live.
You can't go back to the splendor in the grass, but can make it stay, sometimes sing.

Written from 1/23/2023 to 1/26/2023

Summon skeletons all you want, but this is not the goal, Necromancers only exist to fools who can summon the dead back to earth, the one true goal is to live forever, everyone wants immortality. Anything that has been imagined is possible, in this era, we know this to be true, even if for now just digitally in certain movies. Necros live to raise more of what's dead, including forums online and their message. Suspended animation is not the goal, unless we can live in a virtual realm that is kept going by those who are still fully conscious, that is until perhaps robots or cyborgs can manage that system solid. The scary thing is robots making robots. This system would link everyone together on earth (and elsewhere) like the Internet does. One day that'll happen, and there will be less sorrow.

We humans are like the trees that grow on our planet, we all attract different birds as they, bear different fruits, some sour some sweet some poisonous and some that are unique. We are built for others sometimes, but we all need some alone time too, to remember what we've done, where we're going. Like dreaming; something that happens when we're asleep. Awake to a dream and you know what it means, they are symbolic depending on the scene, representing what it means to be free, or perhaps just to exist to be, maybe others telling us something through them, a conduit in the darkness of sleep. The voices we hear when we first rest, calling our name – it's not the trance of sleep but the entry into that gateway where we breathe and see those who maybe show they care as intrusive as it may be. Defrag the mind when you sleep, clean up and organize your totality, value it, protect it, set aside time every night to prepare yourself for your sleep, enjoy it most of all, it's nice to relax into a dream, or something you gathered during the day or night, ask the reasons why you need to do this thing, or why you do not need to, either way it's your personal private comfortable space, a place for you to rejuvenate, to think of things you create, but don't let yourself hate, that only brings bad feelings inside, but challenges in the greater tongue ravage another soul, touche to another sometimes means nothing to another role. Malice in dislike becomes physical, so avoid and use coping skills if you dislike those you find playing those roles. Wear a mask not too heavily, or the monster you become. All trolls in the real and in alterspace, the future internet of sorts are just flirting with others you see, unless they're sad and alone, or just plain jittery, they try to fish for details because their life may lack luster or a proper home.

Trolls are out of touch in the real, their time on earth to condemn others for their own misgivings, to search and try to find a way to learn through others they become sappers of knowledge to quiet their empty selves, or just that they cannot connect properly as they've been told.

Tears are valid, they are your personal weep, the seed that touches off the hope and care of future dream, to be a valve for sadness, a turn off of what you bleed, to end your pain and suffering through crying brings you better thoughts to please, to set you at ease. Tears are an undying communication intercepted, something inside you feed, a build up of sadness over various things. But remember to cry when it happens, don't hold back either on your dreams. Which is just a nice way of saying you must be all you can be, we're all doing our best for each moment, for it's all we can do you see.

Being yourself is something you can do with time, and you get better and better at it because it is all inside, no one else is there – don't be afraid to look within for every answer, because with yourself you should share. Keeping a secret with yourself is the best practice for keeping other's secrets as well. You can't out do others only what you yourself do well, it's not competition though that's what you seek, remember camaraderie is more important with others and yourself instead of beating them at their game.

Your life matters, the monks faraway in the snow of Tibet say, a human life is a very rare thing among the stars, the planets and celestial bodies of every thing. Mass and density is important, every drop of matter in space though it may seem infinite, is finite to what we see. Infinity exists if we live forever but begin by making it matter, so this life counts to ourselves most of all, because others have their limits in this one holistic dream of reality. There is more space out there than matter, like the Tao Te Ching says we need to make things work, like the space between spokes in a wheel, or the room in a vase, it's the space in a house that makes it inhabitable, but fill it with the wrong kinds of babble, the bad kind of murk where families can become split up because of what is said, mere sound that can hurt. All the space in the world we have, there is not much matter in the galaxies, just an empty endless highway off of our planet, to a star faraway that may be the end of our kind and our breed. The matter that matters is us, and how we treat one another, our environments and our realm within, be good to your fellow man and woman, boy and girl, no matter how you feel, because vengeance takes place first in the heart, but almost always in some way big or small tries to sadly and wrongfully kill.

Remember there is only one you, unique, for all time on earth among the sages and kings, just one of you can be. And only one other too, when you get to the right age, behind one man in humans is a woman, a successful man, a good woman who lives to love him with her all, to bring out the best in that man instead of an empty wintry squall. If a woman loves, she shows it, it cannot hide. She called me a shovel-head in my youth, yet I loved her with my all, it was empty love because I never loved her in reality, just in my head carrying a torch for empty years I cared for her soul. Sun or rain I would go to her supposed home after school, plucking roses I would leave them for her, the days took their toll. A notice that read: "Kim doesn't live here but thanks for the flowers anyway". I walked a lonely road down the street, a car passed by and saw my plight, laughing at me and misunderstanding why, and I took the last rose and crushed it, sad and frustrated, on the hard cold concrete there it lie, smashed into smithereens with my loneliness inside, I later found out she lived there where that last rose lay splashed on that street in the mid 90's, I couldn't believe this as why. How could that girl live there where I crushed that rose, I know not in sigh. If she knew the story she'd probably shun me and just say she only wrote that love letter because of her shallow side, we only talked for one hour on the phone, then left me alone. You can feel love inside for someone or something, but if it never comes back my son, then let it not reciprocate. But don't let that get in the way. Love it as much as you want, for it will grow, till it gets dark and then upon you it does sorrowfully take it's toll. It is that wintry edition of the soul, the things you write will become tenebrous and you will yearn with all your low feelings that call.

But gloom is a way into inspiration, don't be fooled. Love is the best for sure, but it's a kingdom that is never ruled. A place for both, never one. And never won. But never will your heart be soothed, unless it is true love, which rarely happens for us, only in fantasy is it true. At least to my eyes and my life, it has only gone this way, sadly I could have been worthy of love. But now my life ages me older now and with grey. To face my life now alone is my greatest test, to be alone the rest of my life is how I feel like that rose pitifully forsaken on that cold hard ground which long ago I laid to rest. Infinite beauty for one small moment in time, and thoughts like these seal my fate. A rose in endless beauty never reached the girl I thought was the same. I tire of these moments in time. Empty forsaken love, that's all my life has been, empty and endlessly sad, worrisome for me as I get old. A plan is all I can contrive, or a semblance to one, and keep all my dead feelings and sadness inside, without a partner, just tears that make me within realize that time is stealing me away. I could write volumes of sadness in love that had never been. My truth is thus, do not live this way, find someone who cares my son, because your heart will sway, let it have it's way, you cannot go back to the splendor in the grass, but you can make it stay.

Pressure makes a diamond - in the human soul, a seed – for future harvests your mind can gather, to guide and reap. Experience sums up a life as long as it isn't lived in shame. Toxic will needs to wither, along with resentment and anger, they must all be banished to the inner flame, where all your strife meets its end, but not to burn long and slow but fast and cold. Feel your feelings, allow yourself room to breathe, deep breathing is always best, meditation is the same. Connection to the breath, mind focused to the point, one pointed to this test, to relax and withdraw within to sense the inner rest. Be at peace within, know what it is truly in your whole being. Like playing the piano in an empty room, only with yourself, a sonata without meaning. It matters to you is what matters in the end, did you enjoy your orchestrated concert with all your powers of creating beautiful song playing? Even though you were alone, it surely helps the test, to be truly comfortable in your own skin, to know what is beautiful by just hearing, and listen, notes fading, but each a reminder we are alone in the ending. Others may even hear, spying at the beauty through the walls around you, but you built them for yourself especially, to guard yourself and your life, even saying that the notes were only for your own pleasing. But what wonderment it is to be the unknown mystery, a maestro of the sonata, a beautiful atramentous yearning. A conductor of a grand symphony, in yourself with your hands and heart and soul, your part leads the whole band, where is it going? Sound that leaps off the walls returning to their master, you must feel these things with your entire being. Don't be ashamed just because others have told you what they think. Be real with yourself, not another's opinion. Life is long, not as short as the futile say, but in your experience, this concert must go on every day.

Boundaries created crossed are the ones others don't always know, even when they know you well. Those who care will respect them, others don't. But in their minds they see it different with little room to spare, because they choose to see it this way, or because it's not their way, or perception in clarity with nowhere to go. Others just don't want to be wronged, and we live our lives to secure ourselves where we go. We all want to live long.

Making plans is important, you cannot always see the way, adventure is important, to keep living every day. But life needs steadiness, a skillful hand, a time to be with yourself sometimes, to ponder at the desires in your mind, what pleases you inside. Your wants. You must feel, as we are human, though remember all life on earth has them though they don't express it, so before you crush that spider remember what it hunts. Webs are made with intentions beforehand, so don't get caught up in them unless you are surefooted in your earthly haunts. Skill is half poignancy, a quarter will, and a spontaneity that thrives in action in the moment, at the bleeding edge of your time. It is on the spot, impromptu, creative much. Skill makes you appreciate what you can do with your own two hands, that sing a chorus in amazing lofty ideas in dream, that become real with the creators hands, that will into existence a million things.

Inspiration will come to you when beauty sees to it that you will not be alone in your willingness to cope. That you are better within for wanting to hope, for challenging others but making right yourself, regardless of what has been said, you must have integrity and inner wealth. Be kind to yourself, be good to what is there; regardless of your station in life, you exist if not in duty or meaning to others, but your own ways.

Quality time is the best ever spent; your interpretation of this is based on what you feel is what is comfortable, enjoyable, and attractive for your own way, and find what is meaningful in your time, something that puts you at ease, whether its collecting music, to have laughter at jokes which all are certain dualities, or to deep breathe. I listen to music to inspire and feel certain ways, like right now as I write, the music to "The Last Samurai" plays. Time is created for yourself and others, try not to falter, but above all, keep your word to others. What kind of man are you if you can't keep your word? It must be said with meaning and a promise you'll do the above. Whether you pass the time sewing rugs or hunt the deer to make those, involve yourself to the fullest, a Zen like trance will occur; your thoughts and inspirations can be marvelous and an enduring path will verve. The communication between inspiration and enlightenment is called this, that Zen I speak. Rehearse your goals and dreams, and gallantly stride into them now and again, the things you want to be, or see, taste, touch, or hear, perhaps even meet. Life is rich; a full bounty of a variety of tastes, they say variety is the spice of life, it surely is an interesting one to live, your tastes will change over time and that's O.K. just make sure you hold the path you've set, and if you stray, the adventure is taking a detour unto other realms you will stay.

When you focus on anything important, try to see if your passion follows, when you work hard it pays off later but laziness pays off now as we wallow. If your passion is there, so your interest and want will be. You'll just love spending time with what you find, things that keep your attention, a curiosity and intense attraction, this is the key. What you love in the particular frame of mind you act in, the kind of thinking or mode of thought that you truly do adore will set you free. Put yourself in others shoes sometimes to see. The wise man learns from himself, but the wiser one from others deeds. Pay attention to your needs, get them met in the honest way you can, not at others expense, but your own willing hand. Be a kind of self made man. Sometimes compromise and opportunity enables others to help, mostly because they're getting paid. Time is not money; money is just a means to an end, your time on earth is so much more valuable than dollars and rupees and yen.

To write well, the swordplayer would say, is that the pen is mightier than the sword, and you can actually control what you have to make easier than a blade. Violence is never forgotten, it is a stain on a reputation, a tarnished mark of dishonor among those who physically lay hands on others in their way. You must determine that the moment at hand is important in your life now and always, and see clear the reasons for your own suffering, where it leads your pain. The decisions and choices of a quick succession of moments determine the honor of a thousand years they say. Try to be fair to others, remember the golden rule, do unto others as they do unto you. Just because they do something to you wrong does not mean you must be mutual in that dance and song, try to accept gracefully what has been taken or given, and be clear of troubles on your own. Respect is a natural thing, that takes time. You can destroy a good reputation in seconds of life. Be wary of others who you feel or sense are trouble, regardless of what is said of them by those you know, our first impression or sense of something or someone is our best judgement call.

Use just a small amount of toothpaste on your brush, it doesn't take much. Brush all your teeth carefully and not too hard, brush your gums too, and the tongue side of your teeth well. Don't miss any surface, and floss between your teeth down to the gums, wiggle the floss over both parts of where they meet in your mouth, to dislodge any food particles breaking down, that inevitably will rot your fangs if not taken care of. Use non alcohol mouthwash if you must, but brushing and flossing come first. Brush your teeth once a day, floss at least twice a week or daily if disciplined in habit, to make sure when you floss the gums don't bleed, which is a sign of infection, pay heed. When your teeth are growing in, leave them be. Always respect your teeth, a fine priceless porcelain they are and only one set you keep. It may be hard to smile at times, but an inward one can suffice for you, and keep you happy.

Food these days in this time is prepared for us ready to eat usually. Wrapped or packaged, preserved or canned, you must not eat food that is over-processed, something more fresh you deserve, like fruit and vegetables of which you will learn they are high in fiber, and healthy vitamins and minerals that your body needs replacing every day on this sojourn. Fasting cleanses the body, but you must not do it if on medications, and you must break the fast with certain foods specifically. Eating is a great pleasure in this world, watching your weight will be something you must control. By portions, eating smaller amounts of vittles, so that you do not become over weight as it is unhealthy for your being as a whole. Two thousand or so calories for a man per day we are told. Eat a lot of mono and polyunsaturated fats, found in avocados, olive oil, of which you should use extra virgin cold pressed, and be sure you don't heat it too much, it's best if you pour it as a dressing on salads with lettuce or spinach, it has super things in it which keep you living your best. VOLGGH was my acronym I made, it stands for Vinegar, Olive oil, Lemon, Ginger, Garlic, and Honey. Stay away from Partially Hydrogenated Vegetable Oils and Saturated Fat, keep them out of your body. Eat carotenoids found in orange, yellow, and red fruits and vegetables, and polyphenols in red or purple ones. You want to consume lots of phytochemicals in your diet, and sometimes sit for a few minutes a day in the sun, but not too much. Drink tea not coffee, have some matcha green tea to indulge in some EGCG (epigallocatechin gallate), and dark chocolate with high cocoa percent which is good for you, don't chew but let it dissolve, melting in your mouth, enjoying it is what it's all about. Eat a handful or two of mixed nuts a day, their protein and trace minerals keep you going with raw energy, keeping you in the fray. Sushi tastes great, though I never had raw fish, I'd make it myself, with avocado and cooked rainbow trout. You will start to love certain foods more than others, but stay away from sugar and salt in packets. You will crave the raw goodness of fruits just as blueberries, mangoes, bananas, kiwi, pineapple, and oranges. They say three main meals a day to keep you healthy, but smaller meals with ones between is just as good a habit.

Learn to cook for yourself wherever you dwell, it is cheaper, healthier, and tastier this way, and more proud you will become. Even if you have no one to cook for, cook for yourself. Start soups from scratch, use a pressure cooker to automate the task. Blend smoothies into sweet delicious drinks that are mind-blowingly healthy and rad. Banana and milk, either soy, oat, almond, or cow make a good base for these drinks you'll build and enjoy to have. Perfect the spices and herbs in your dishes and you will master the art of the chef. The sauces and marination matter the most when preparing meat, I hope you'll love the flavor of garlic the best.

Food was one of my few pleasures when I walked on the earth, I tended to be alone in my search. Try in your life to not be lonely my son. Why did I need to create you with what I held an animosity for? The female creature is something though I tended to hate, I did at one time truly adore, even though I walked alone myself, even at the beach by the seashore. If you cannot share your time with an effeminate being, don't unto yourself deplore. It can tear away at your soul. Try to manage your time well. And be effective and try to be somewhat happy with what you know. Not so much though with what you own. I learned to pack light in all scenarios, keeping only necessities with me, other things became mere conversation pieces I'd much rather sell on Amazon or give to the Goodwill for free.

Rivalry creates a mystique of motivational curiosity, an intellect and creativity born like a phoenix rising, the nemesis is more than an opponent or enemy, they have their own circles where they dwell and act and fight. The rival creates a pact of dislike, though from this, numerous insights. A bond made strong from a shared enemy does not make it right. Surefooted soldiers without weaponry, warriors vast in pen and paper, brush and easel, creating phantasms from their battling ghosts, creating images and inspirations from them that take notes and canvas coats, of many colors we make the new come alive, created inside, becoming rows of grain towards the rising sun, any kind of art becomes our grandest home, a symphony of our own, our sacred rite for those who travel the depths of the soul.

Being professional doesn't always mean playing a role, it's handling everything well, being knowledgeable in your field, having grace and leadership when the weather takes its toll. Insurance doesn't cover everything, especially the incidents they call acts of god. To recover from a disaster, to build back up to where you were once again, an entrepreneur in spirit, a firm shake of the hand. Keeping it professional is always a good choice, you may not be able to throw a charm; but being just with integrity is what can be best about how you are. A good leader follows others it is said, professional attitude follows with this, be transparent with how you're being read.

Respect your time, spend it well, it is the essence of life, invisible, but space can see beyond this reality, a place inside. We only have so much energy in our time. In this life you must remember, you are original, not a snowed in beast, though the world has so many dangers, you may have to lurk to breathe. When you walk across the street, always twice look both ways. By the time you can read this son, perhaps you'll already know, and I hope you stay free of them, but stay away from drugs, they will ruin and wreck your soul, drain your money, and hurt others in the process of using any of them at all. Substances will destroy your life, this I have seen of others. Know that I've never touched any of them at all, lucky in this sense I am, but they are a bane on humanity, a way of destroying ourselves. My mother taught me that it's your willpower to keep them away, and not to let others who do them in at all. Friends who offer these things are not looking at your best interests in life. Avoid or help, because they are walking on thin ice. Perhaps too involved in that abyss to know any better, be careful who you call a friend in your time, and best friends are rare to be sure, especially the ones that call, so cherish the time you have with them, nothing is forever after all. Be supportive of your friends, guide them in the right direction, good counsel is worth much when others struggle even with depression. We are cosmic visitors at this age in my life I tend to think and say, so appreciate the moments you have with others who wish you well on your way.

Emotion Identifying
Now sandbox or quarantine and separate from emotion
Discover the root of emotion
Enough time to give the emotion and thoughts some work
Alternative thoughts or avoid
Very much love thyself
Order and build the habit of an upward spiral
Resolve to end suffering

I worry about things in the end that don't matter; things that chide me within till I inside shatter. A lot of time spent alone, things kept inside when I should be rhyming like Post Malone. One day I'll be free again to live at my own whim. To choose my own path and when worry strikes let it go again. Most of my worries don't even count in the end. Live happy, free as a bird, but now no more messages to send. To go back to a home I don't live in anymore, I have not to settle a score. I have more passions now I adore. Time spent free as this, even when totally free, we're all doing time, especially when we're lonely. Enjoying my time in quality time, no worries for now, but when did they truly exist, they never did. A delusional illusion of things bantered on about, things surprisingly kept inside. For what did I need to rid, just enjoy your time is all I've really said.

So, I wrote a song called "Stay", 4/22/2015

Now I would just stay there alone
Following direction of the soul
Stay oh ya stay, going in the direction that I go
The direction that I roam
I just stay, centered in the middle of abyss,
Only soothing sleepy soul
Stay there alone, stay there alone, staying up alone
Climbing heights I did solo, with no hand to ever hold
Staying, staying alone
Staying, staying gone
Stay
In the middle of abyss of blue woe, making sand castles of the
soul
Tides drifting, creations of my love
Stay still alone, stay there stay
Icy abyss of soul so long
Icy abyss I call on icy abyss alone
An icy abyss now in woe
Stay in the sun to melt without

Beneath the ice, many fathoms deep lay a beautiful princess asleep. Being like a ship sunken to the bottom of the sea; a ghost roaming the hull among no family, she rested in her dreams.

The past is dead; one yet many futures ahead. Destiny in time awaits. No sorrow or fear going to my head. This greatest test I must face, racing to disgrace memories erased, forcing worries out in haste. Working on posture, integrity of the soul's base. To taste the efficacy of life's twisting maze, puzzles in mystery to find the destiny that awaits. I am not my crime, I did my time, I will be free. I am safe, I am happy, no more illness, plenty more of life to see.

Slay me, put me beyond the suffering of silence
Slay me quick with words, that echo from that sweetest voice in my heart that I've known.
Slay me with mercy, because I loved. Don't drift in the wind forever silent, slay my soul with the sound of rain, the sun of times past, no pain but love.
Slay the soul thinking you were its one.

In my waking hours I see the outside sun. Time glimmering, a way to get things done. To enjoy what little is left of existence, even if existence means many thousands of tomorrows, the heart's path adrift, with suffering and no love, even if.

You're unwanted, undeserving of love, you write poems that are sad to curse the stars above, you wait and get old, and treat yourself rough. Wake up within, understand that's not how it's so. When you just live to enjoy it all and not suffer in my flow, how expansive my own personal universe could be in soul. I'm not immortal, I'm here as long as thou, I better write less tenebrous and try to some day find true love.

A jingle for "Kuryu Chan", 8/18/2007

When I see a dream then I lose it all
And I hunt for the pain when I feel it within and in a fantasy of
love I've never known, and In my mind and my spirit and my
flesh and my soul
But my body, but my body will never know oh oh oh oh oh oh
Heaven only knows, only my mind knows, not my body, my
body and soul ohooh
Kuryu Chan is the land I spread all my owns upon
Everything I own, all my possessions and soul,
Everything with you is Kuryu Chan, Kuryu Chan

Another song I wrote called "Lonely Solo Mage", 3/12/2021

They say I've got the hands of a magician
But I can't make you appear
This vision alone in twilight insincere
This life alone, this life alone, so cold, no hold, no role, no soul,
no more, no more

I've lived it solo for so long, I've been alone in my own abyss
With no one to miss, with no one to live
My life is mine I must admit, but my time is empty without
your kiss

My only wish, my empty sitch,
My empty days on this world's lost river of Styx.
Charon you must wait, even the river boatman is a lone myth
Gently gently flowing to Hades
Gently flowing to Hades

My lost empty youth was a corpse run,
playing games in life's lost maze; EQ became a thing
All I could end up doing on RZ was PK.

I've lived it solo for so long, I've been alone in my own abyss
With no one to miss, with no one to live
My life is mine I must admit, but my time is empty without
your kiss

The hands of a mystic mage or SK, youth disappearing now
into old age, fading away

I've lived it solo for so long, I've been alone in my own abyss
With no one to miss, with no one to live
My life is mine I must admit, but my time is empty without
your kiss

Broken   3/20/2021

I could never find the love that I seek, heartbroken in my
dreams. Suffering so silently in every way, every day, like it's
here to stay. Nothing ever comes back my way. Inside I fade
away. Antiquated memory, unsweet, somber sadness chaining
me, make me free. Let me leave. This place echoes inside of
me. How could love turn to hate when it never could be? Why
is it something I still seek? Drowning in the river of tears
carrying me to the sea. It makes me old, ancient smiles unfree.
Old and gray, unloved to the end where I die one day, for all
time, that time drifting lost, sad, and repressed, unready to
face death in my lonely quest. Soul facing its greatest test in
unrest, broken solo in a mess of sad regret. Searching the spirit
and finding the new me I've met. Refreshed by emptiness,
enthusiasm, and nothing left. Never finding any love to seek, a
broken life somewhere in the sea, jagged coral reefs, lunar
light leading me. A broken raft crashing, almost sinking to
waves, sleeping heartbroken in my dreams.

Have gratitude for what you have, though I know you won't know me. At age 43 I came back to an empty place with my whole family dead; possessions that meant nothing in the end, not a woman in sight to love or wed, not a friend to hold in hand. Just pictures of a past in albums covered with dust. Treated them with respect but many things in the past are just that, tears or rust. Organizing things kept by my father's friend from the north, after my father died, I finally received the old belongings I will just not keep anymore in my strife. That man, my father, tended to be mean, he drank himself to sleep, my mother controlled the scene. They fought too much as did I, for most of my time living with their deeds. They did raise me well though I must say. I got a good social personality from her, though in my future I had no one to share it with, no one close to me. Work on yourself my son, in the meantime, love yourself unless you have something better to do or see. Just because you are alone in the world among the many billion others on earth, it is a fact you will be living like a curse; find your worth. Find an interest, something productive you see, something to keep you living, because you can live under that dying tree, which you'll chop down eventually, and it only becomes a seat, but never a seed, at least visibly, a new tree with roots for feet and limbs with leaves, we sprout and die leaving inner soul, and venture out into the unknown, to the Gardens of Greece, or the Pharaohs of Egypt, where shall we go? Read my other book too, son, so you know where I'm coming from. Tenebrous Yearning, a book of poetry from my own lone soul, a time you may suffer as me, but may that tree shade you from the worst of what I've had to endure, I pray you have someone to keep closer, someone to love and with happier life concur.

Enjoy the nature of this beauteous world, no matter how long we live, we can never fully have enough time to take in it all. Poetry and rhyme are out there, within your weeping and trying times, but you have to go experience it, to adventure into the wilds, find the rhyme in your life. It comes together easier than you know or think, many things rhyme with each other, you just have to be. The silence is important in life, to enjoy those moments when the quietude sinks deeply in your soul, to meditate and find within that precious seed, that plants answers to what you deeply seek, your wishes become real in reality, you will not notice the ones that end up becoming real in the end, because they are deeply sewn within. Deeply seated seeds that grow and break the earth you have to tend.

Keep the power inside, my mentor Osiris said. Letting it go when you know you have to accomplish something, saying it to others, may keep you from doing it when you are better off keeping it as a soulseed. You will accomplish many great things alone, don't let new mountains to climb be a stymied approach to where you go, team means together everyone achieves more, but by yourself if you're cunning and sharp, you are better than many men times your own. Many of them together cannot feel like one, or even feel the things you need to feel to get something very interesting or inspirational done. They're split among each other, if you can handle this on your own independently, autonomously, most of the tasks you've then won. Be crafty, take things apart and put them together again how they fit, seeing how they work on the inside within. I usually just used my materia from Final Fantasy 7 called Ifrit. They say think outside the box, but you'll never do that till you know what's in it. Sephiroth was my favorite villain, the story in that game was great. Video games can be timesinks but they put you on another level of leisure in this world, to escape. One of my favorite pastimes, in the modern day, they help me to dream, to relieve me of fate, keeping me fulfilled and enjoying the life of a gamer is relaxing, a new way to see things.

An Aunt passed away in the northern part of the state, relating to my father around Christmas day, a time we would visit her yearly and stay. My father said, "There are three whole generations sitting in this room today". She knew her time was coming to a close, she lost her husband months before. She wanted to be buried in a place faraway in Iowa, with her father who died many years ago. The time came when she passed in her sleep, Dear Aunt Louise, and upon hearing this, went back to her, we took her across thirteen states, and it was quite the trip, we set her in the ground, in a graveyard of old stone on one side, and granite headstones on the other, one said, "Killed by Indians 1845". We searched every grave, and finally found where her father was. The groundskeeper came, and told my father he could be put in chains. He kept patting down the place where she was laid to rest with his entrenching tool, and he gave my dad a break. We learned from two in that old faraway town that the grass grew over where my precious Aunt now sleeps. It was a long trip we took, I saw the Alamo on my birthday, it wasn't planned; being named after the Colonel who defended it in 1836 by William Barrett Travis. My father was a man of honor for completing this task, I saw much of the states, many a presidents grave, including Lincolns; a dark, cold mausoleum, an eerie place. A good man he was, big into historical facts, though a quiet disposition, silence is what he wanted mostly in his presence, I miss my dad and wonder what journeys we could have had should he had lived, though now it's all reminiscence. Once we drove north and he said, "It's the ghost of old Indian Joe, he leaves no trails in the snow for he walks between the winds".

I took one or two fishing trips with my father a long time ago, we caught no fish, a river of no hope. On coming back, he said to me, "We've gone on great trips together, but when I die that is the trip I have to take alone." Remember who is close. That they matter to you, try to tell them how you feel. We all have different riches in this life, but for me other people this close were few. If I could have one more talk with that man or my mother, it could end up as an argument, so don't regret what is done in time, it had meaning at the moment, it was the most you could do, despite wishing you could reach them just once more in life. When the day comes you have to part ways, remember your choices, your feelings you had, visceral and raw, apart of you and they, more words sometimes just are what keep you both at bay. I dreamed of my father before he had passed when I was locked away in a hospital, it was a dark rainy night on a bus line headed for some unknown destination, we were standing there, my dad poured coins in my hand slowly, saying to me "you may need them one day". I remembered when I was real young, playing at the arcades at the mall, he gave me quarters to play the games. That is the way we reflected on a happy time, perhaps a gift from him through the dreamworld to remember again, to bring back what was good in life. I miss them sometimes, and knowing where my life goes now, my quarters are all gone. It's what you've given to others that goes on.

I've never written letters that I've never sent, to write them once with heart, perhaps repent, or send something to a person you'll never know again, and never give them what you meant, but these pages written are to you my son, that I'll never get to meet. Girls were always wrong to me, they could never beget my seed, could never talk even well with me, poisonous, they never ask an innocent question, my story is too sad for any of them to hear or see. There is no other way you could come to this earth, the Aghora 1, At left hand of god among the books I read, as a dear brother of faith one man called me, though I just wanted to chant myself into oblivion, to go invisible in mantra chanting with my unanswered quandary. The law of karma perhaps could bid me well, though I've created hells for myself. I do not know what lies beyond the gates, lions of stone that roar fate, that will open soon in time, wealth is empty if all you have is your own rhyme, tempting your way. In "The Legend of Ton Po", a story I wrote a long time ago, a monk went against an undead dragon, past the point of no return, when he knew everything he loved was gone. Now that feels like me. We become mixed up too heavily in our lines of our roles. Life imitates Art more than vice versa I've heard.

With age, wisdom, the beauty fades aside, the depth of the wrinkles become the legended page, an abyss of time. Questions deep as the elden ones so far yet silent in life. Knowing in silence, passing on the written page, wrinkles made like canyons where endless tears once fell like rivers, creating sages through the pain. The shell that encloses understanding, reasons why the beauty fades.

Something is sacred by how you treat it, an Apache friend once said. A great mission in a desert land had a chapel near the cloister end, I stepped within it's confines in the moist wooden-smelling darkness, a hundred candles aflame, a place where others meet and shed their travails, with spirit free, like my friend. I was touched with holy water by my dad, from a stone fountain, old and worn from use by many monks and others seeking to cleanse sin. The rafters went high in this old church looking room, wooden beams high up and frescoes along the old and worn walls where the candles bounced shadows that illuminated the whole scene. A certain holiness I found in this place, never have I experienced a calm feeling such as this, simple and serene. I return to that moment, not for sadness or to seek poignance, but to know the innocence, the spirit of sacredness, the calm grave behind the place with the name "Diego" I kept what lay upon the tomb, a seed.

Your life has just begun, no matter your age. Welcome to the first day of the rest of your life, treat yourself with care, and others without hate or rage. Be kind to them, they're trying to get by just as you; they like you must exist to change. Evolution in my writing this, for it only took three days. I ask you to not worry, though your concerns have a valid say. The wind will take you far wherever you wish to go, remember who you are, a prayer keep you safe. You don't have to meet others to put on the same show. They know you through the silence revered alone. When we die, we need not make a scene, funerals are for the living, our time here on earth should be lived free. Be happy; do not live to seethe, we'll all be forgotten one day, even by our bereaved. I just want to be walking with my father again along that beautiful coast, instead of taking a picture of him walking like a ghost in the distance in the coldness of the air of the north; to just be with him there, not out of touch. That nail we found buried in the sand may indeed be from Magellan's ship like he said of it, always use your imagination or it will rust. And now he fades into my indelible memory; the lighthouse finds our ship ashore. Maybe one day it will go to sea once more.

-T. F. Lanning

Made in the USA
Columbia, SC
15 July 2023

20076198R00024